Penmanship

Of the XVI, XVII & XVIIIth centuries

A series of typical examples from English and

foreign writing books

Lewis F. Day

Alpha Editions

This edition published in 2019

ISBN : 9789353898557

Design and Setting By
Alpha Editions
email - alphaedis@gmail.com

PENMANSHIP

OF THE XVI, XVII & XVIIIth CENTURIES

OTHER WORKS BY LEWIS F. DAY

ALPHABETS OLD AND NEW.   Third Edition
LETTERING IN ORNAMENT
PATTERN DESIGN
ORNAMENT AND ITS APPLICATION
NATURE AND ORNAMENT
ART IN NEEDLEWORK.   Third Edition
ENAMELLING
WINDOWS: A BOOK ABOUT STAINED
& PAINTED GLASS.   Third Edition

BY PERCY J. SMITH
LETTERING AND WRITING.
               A Portfolio of Examples

Alturas. Camino. Decio.
Estim. Emerit. Famosa
Glorioso. Hermoso. Justi
Kaul. Luminoso. Luz.
Montes. Naturalmen-
Qrror. Poblar. Quinien-
Reglam. Solv. Vestir.
Trans. Utilissimo. Virg.
Xavier. Yglesia. Zerri-

Palomares, Madrid, 1789

PENMANSHIP

OF THE XVI, XVII & XVIIIth CENTURIES

A series of typical Examples from English
and Foreign Writing Books selected by

LEWIS F. DAY

Author of " Alphabets Old and New "
" Lettering in Ornament" "Windows" etc.

JEAN
DE LA
CHAMBRE
Scribe

FROM A
PAINTING
BY FRANS
HALS, 1638.

LONDON

B. T. BATSFORD, 94 HIGH HOLBORN

[191-?]

NOTE BY MISS DAY

PENMANSHIP has, of recent years, assumed a position of so great importance as a branch of art education that there is no need to make any apology for bringing out a book on the subject. The present volume, moreover, deals with a branch of penmanship which has been practically ignored of late, and about which little has been written. The tendency has been to pay little attention to any kind of lettering but uncial, half-uncial, and Roman. But, whilst the dignity of these letters must be apparent to every one, there are purposes for which they are quite unsuitable, and it is for just these purposes that the lightness and comparative frivolity of more modern writing is peculiarly well adapted.

While going through an important collection of Writing Books of the 16th, 17th, and 18th centuries, at that time in the possession of Mr. Batsford, it occurred to my father that here was a very mine of suggestions for the inspiration of writers, illuminators, architects, engravers, and the numerous art workers who have to use lettering in one form or another.

Mr. Batsford's collection, which has been largely drawn upon for this volume, contained a number of rare old writing books, not to be found at the British Museum or in the Library of the Victoria and Albert Museum. We have, however, not been content with simply reproducing these; we have gone through hundreds of writing books—Dutch, English, French, German, Italian, Portuguese, and Spanish—in order that we may be able to give not only a representative collection of hand-writings, but the best possible examples. In examining this mass of material, we were astonished to find how much of it, though finely engraved, was quite unsuitable to modern needs. We discovered, further, that the later writing masters were in the habit of calmly copying from their predecessors (though they don't usually mention the fact) and vulgarizing their work in the process, so that from one cause or another a good many of the most easily accessible writing books are really worthless to the student.

My father had, before his death, chosen most of the ex-amples now reproduced, the remainder have been added by Mr. Percy J. Smith, Mr. Batsford, and myself; and we have closely followed his principles of selection, and have adhered in the main to his plan of arrangement. Our special thanks are due to Mr. C. L. Ricketts of Chicago, who has most readily offered suggestions as to the volumes best worth referring to. We have also to thank the authorities of the British Museum and the Victoria and Albert Museum for permission to repro-duce certain plates.

It is not contended that all the pages given are altogether admirable, or that everything, or indeed anything, in the volume should be copied as it stands. What we have tried to do is, to provide students, teachers, and craftsmen with good examples of penmanship which may serve to show them what has been done, and what can be done, with a pen, and to inspire them to attempt something of their own which may be dis-tinctive and graceful without necessarily being too far removed from the writing of everyday life.

With regard to the arrangement of the plates, writing masters used such varying terminology that it was hopeless to try to group the examples after the manner of any particular penman, whilst to arrange them in a strictly chronological order would have meant simply chaos. It has therefore been necessary to try some rather different plan. The book begins with some examples of the various Chancery hands, and these are followed by specimens of Old English, German, Roman, and other more or less formal types of penmanship. The rather restrained running hands come next, followed, in their turn, by writing characterized by more or less heavy blobs of ink at the ends of the letters. The current hands in which flourishes are predominant, bring to an end the examples chosen simply as writing. The remaining illustrations contain a few specimens of how title-pages and other special work were set out and framed up, and some examples of scrolls and flourishes.

The book does not pretend to be in any sense a history of penmanship—that would be a very large undertaking—but those interested in calligraphy, from a more or less antiquarian point of view, will find a good deal of information in the list of books from which the illustrations have been taken, whilst the wants of the more strictly practical student have been provided for by the descriptive list of plates.

R. M. D.

SHORT CRITICAL NOTES ON PENMANSHIP WITH REFERENCE TO THE EXAMPLES IN THIS WORK, BY PERCY J. SMITH

DURING the 16th, 17th, and 18th centuries Penmanship, *i.e.* the *style* or *manner* of writing, occupied a position in the curriculum of studies which it is difficult for us to appreciate to its full extent: its practitioners and professors were often men of culture and influence, and held a very high place in the esteem of their contemporaries. Among these we may mention, as a representative English scribe, John Davies of Hereford. Educated at Oxford University, and pursuing his occupation as writing master in the same city, he was very well known during the late 16th and early 17th centuries both as a poet and as one of the most skilful penmen of his day. His epigrams and sonnets, containing references to Shakespeare, Fletcher, Ben Jonson and other writers of the period, show the calligrapher to have been on terms of friendship with many of his most notable contemporaries. At one time he had many pupils in Magdalen College, and drew others, including Algernon, Lord Percy, from families of the highest rank. One of his pupils, Richard Gething, who worked at the sign of the *Hand and Pen* in Fetter Lane, London, also attained considerable eminence at a little later date.

The work of the best of the penmen deserves study, not only because we find reflected in it the spirit of their time, but because, if we put aside their exaggerated displays of technical skill and "ingenuity in making divers curious figures," for theirs is essentially a conscious art, we shall find much that is beautiful, fundamentally right, and of practical use in the work of to-day.

It is not possible within the necessarily brief limits of these notes to consider separately all the examples from old writing books here brought together ; moreover, were they thus treated, the interested student would lose somewhat the valuable and pleasurable exercise of personal judgment and discovery. Nor will the relation between the styles or the development of the various characters be investigated, for to treat that part of the subject adequately would require a history of writing. This is an introduction to the collection as a whole ; references will be made to specific examples, but mainly as representative of a particular style or of a method of treatment, while the criticisms made and principles laid down will be found capable of a very wide application. The guiding thought and intention will be *to open the eyes of the mind to perceive the best.*

It is deeply to be regretted that we are deprived of the advantage of the late Mr. Day's experience and trained judgment in the introduction which should rightly be his, for his knowledge of, and interest in, everything appertaining to lettering is too well known to need emphasis here, and it must needs be a source of regret that we cannot know his thoughts and consider his criticism on these examples of the craft. Both before and since his death the collection has passed through many examinations and siftings, and every example contains some feature or features justifying its inclusion ; though occasionally pages are reproduced with details which it is not desirable that we should emulate or study. Especially is this true of the initials, as, for instance, in the work of Beauchesne and Baildon in Example 30, but with the exception of this initial the page well repays study, both for the character displayed in the small letters and for the signs of playfulness in the slight scrolls and flourishes.

At the close of the 15th century a formal literary or book-hand ceased to be generally practised ; it was superseded by the printing press; and it was during the 16th century that cursive writing, under the pressure of influence from the northern Gothic or pointed style and the southern more rounded and freely written Italian script, passed through one of its most interesting phases. This period may be considered to mark the birth of modern writing. The first three examples of this collection, and others of the style of Examples 7 and 8, exhibit very clearly the influence of northern 15th-century bookwork. The letters have much of the "weight" and solidarity of type, while the freedom of penwork is evident in the treatment of descending strokes, and in the use of flourishes and scrolls. Example 4, which is also type-like in character, is taken from a Spanish writing book of the 18th century and shows a style of work noticeable for its fine roundness and bold simplicity of form, combined with good, clear spacing of letters and lines; the value of these qualities in ensuring readability, and what we may define as tranquillity and a forceful serenity of character in the page, cannot easily be overestimated.

The decorative value of a headline of letters, larger and heavier than the text, may be seen in such examples as 11, 18, 20, and 25; while No. 14, an example of work by John Ayres, writing-master in St. Paul's Churchyard during the last half of the 17th century, is worthy of study as suggesting a legitimate method of interlineal decoration forming, as it were, a rich background of pattern or tone which need in no way interfere with the legibility of the matter. The somewhat thin and weak treatment of some of the scrolls and the complete isolation of others are weaknesses we must not repeat in work based upon this example. The page is, however, full of suggestion to metal workers and engravers, of whose craft it is peculiarly reminiscent. The superiority of the wide Gothic writing over the laterally compressed form in such essentials of good lettering as legibility, dignity, and strength, may be studied in Examples 14, 15, and others.

The Italian or Roman style, destined to supersede the heavier and more complicated Gothic, is illustrated in Example 35, a very beautiful piece of late 16th-century work. The initial " D " is well constructed and full of vitality. The student should observe the strength and very beautiful subtlety of form in this letter, especially noting how the bow springs from the base of the stem and, curving well out, returns and completes its form with a slight drop. Observe, too, the honouring of the two important words and the decorative value accruing from the use thus made of the line of capitals ; the equality of weight as between the large and small letters ; the excellent spacing, which is a thing so little understood and so rarely well done in these days ; the freedom with which the lines are allowed to terminate where they will, without excessive spreading out or closing up ; and, lastly, the simplicity and good composition of the whole. All these features combine to make this a very quiet and dignified inscription, severely simple, yet stored with lessons and inspiration for the modern scribe, but even more for the discerning letter-cutter, typographer, and architect.

In Plate 32 we have a small, interesting example of decorative writing from a Spanish copybook of 1650. The arrangement and balance of effect are excellent : and the flourishes are legitimate and unforced accentuations of distinctive parts of the letters from which they spring. They are full of vitality, and while adding interest to the page form a good example of organic decoration. The three lines of small writing are invaluable in providing a base and thus steadying the composition.

Spain has provided us with many examples of a style of calligraphy which, though closely akin to that of Italy, has a distinct national character. Example 49, taken from an 18th-century writing book, is strongly and beautifully written with a slanted pen, and shows an interesting and varied treatment of the serifs or terminating strokes of the *p*'s and *q*'s. Both in this and in other examples, it is well to note that the placing of the dots of the *i*'s is responsible for a feeling of "spottiness." The practice of making the dots range with the tops of the ascending strokes was, and is, often followed, with a resultant loss of connection between the two component parts, and consequent isolation of the smaller member. It adds to the unity of the letter, to the strength of the lines of writing, and to the restfulness of the page, if the dots are placed close to the stems of the letters of which they form necessary parts. It is to be regretted that the border in this example is not in scale with the writing; it is weak in weight of line, and somewhat disconnected in design; nevertheless it contains suggestions as to decoration which should be of practical use to the discriminating student. Another method of adding a decorative interest, and at the same time strengthening the composition of a page which would otherwise be disconnected, is by tying the parts together with bands and lines. These may be judiciously interlaced—as in the two examples from the book of Palatino, one of the earliest and best known of the Italian writing masters, given in Examples 66 and 67.

The very beautiful Italian semi-formal script of the Renaissance had a decisive influence on other European styles, and, mainly as the result of this influence, English cursive writing gradually lost a great part of its disjointed and angular character and acquired the freely written and linked-up manner exemplified in the writing of Peter Gery (see No. 51). Plate 38 and the succeeding italic alphabets and writings are replete with hints to modern workers—witness the interesting and useful forms of amperzands; the character, strength of curvature, and subtleties

of shape and construction in the letters ; the spacing, compact-
ness, and uniformity of the lines ; and the treatment of capitals
and ascending and descending strokes, with their flourishes
and scrolls. The manner of writing the word "Socrates" in
Example 82 is an instructive example of the pride of display
and "ingenuity" of the French penman, Jean de Beaugrand, not
without its fascination for the modern scribe and letter-engraver.
Examples 71 and 72 illustrate good "placing" of title or head-
ing, and the free but fairly reticent rendering of the scrolls in
which the writers loved to show their control of the pen, while
the management of the various items of the note on Plate 74,
written by Maria Strick as a specimen for the guidance of her
numerous pupils, shows a good feeling for balance and composition.

Two varieties of upright writing, both showing good judgment in arrangement, deserve mention. That in Plate 75 has
a pleasing little scroll carried into the lower margin and flanked
and supported by some long vertical lines that materially steady
the design. The other, Plate 90, notwithstanding a rather
heavily inked initial and flourish, exhibits a very beautiful
economy of line in the construction of the letters and suggests
the presence of that restrained power characteristic of most
achievements which win an abiding place in the hierarchy of
things done.

The most delicate writing in the series is that shown in
Examples 80 and 81, selected from a book issued by Beaugrand
early in the 17th century. The graceful and fanciful treatment
of the initials in both examples and of the two scrolls in the
lower margin of the latter is very pleasing and contains ideas for
the modern calligrapher and designer, while in both plates the
judicious placing of the flourishes and consequent accentuation
of the corners greatly strengthens the design as a whole.

The excessively intricate borders so often found in the old

writing books—though they are the inevitable development of the ornamentation of the initials—rarely add to the true beauty of the work and certainly show but little feeling for that restrained power to which reference has just been made. It is sufficient to say here that the examples shown are the most restrained and the best that could be found, and, while they are not to be considered as in any way perfect examples of taste, they are typical of their time and contain suggestions which may be of service.

We are on happier ground when we come to such page arrangements as that of Peter Gery (No. 100). The natural manner in which the arm of the initial L in this plate holds the text, and the steadying influence of the line or base formed by the signature, are vital elements in a very good composition.

A cursory glance through this collection is sufficient to clearly reveal the great importance of the *ensemble* made by the composition. The value of a well-shaped mass—be it light or heavy—as a contribution to the success of a page may be judged by a reference to such examples as 53, 81, and 86. Construction and growth of letter, line, and ornament; steadiness and balance of part against part; the due accentuation of this and the dropping of the other; the question of scale, and the using of ornament, not for its own sake, but to support and give value to the whole; all these considerations are involved in producing a strong and beautiful piece of work and must be remembered while studying these examples.

In conclusion, the writer of this introduction would emphasize, with all due reserve, the supreme importance, in the whole range of Penmanship and Lettering, of an appreciation of reticence combined with legitimate freedom in execution, associated with depth and vitality of spirit in tone and inspiration.

P. J. S.

DESCRIPTIVE LIST OF ILLUSTRATIONS

*For full Titles of the Books quoted, see Alphabetical List of Authors
at the end of this Volume*

1. PAPAL CHANCERY HAND. Spanish, from the Recopilacion Subtilissima of Juan de Yciar, 1548.

2. PAPAL CHANCERY HAND. Italian, from Il Perfetto Scrittore
3. of G. F. Cresci, 1570.

4. A MUCH LATER VERSION OF THE SAME KIND OF HAND. Spanish, from the Arte nueva de Escribir of J. C. Aznar de Polanco, 1719.

5. SET CHANCERY HAND, from A booke containing divers sortes of hands by J. de Beauchesne and John Baildon, 1571.

6. GOTHIC WRITING. Flemish, from the Exercitatio Alphabetica of Clement Perret, 1569.
(Compare Nos. 8, 9, and 14.)

7. GOTHIC WRITING. Netherlandish, from the Exemplaar-Boek of A. Perlingh, 1679.

8. GOTHIC WRITING. Flemish, from the Exemplaria sive Formulae Scripturae Ornatioris XXXIV. of J. Houthusius, 1591.
(Compare Nos. 6, 9, and 14.)

9. GOTHIC WRITING, from the Theatrum Artis Scribendi by J. Hondius. This is a so-called "bastard" English type, and is written by M. Martin, 1594.
(Compare Nos. 6, 8, and 14.)

10. GOTHIC WRITING. Flemish, from the Exemplaer-Boec of J. van den Velde, 1607.

B

11. GOTHIC WRITING, from the Lust-Hof der Schrijft-Konste by Symon de Vries, 1619. Notice the terminations of the *p*'s and *q*'s which are particularly ingenious and the decorative value of the headline.

12. GOTHIC WRITING. German, from the Anweissung zur zierlichen Schreibkunst of B. U. Hoffman, 1694.
(Compare Nos. 11 and 14.)

13. GOTHIC WRITING. English, from A Tutor to Penmanship by John Ayres, 1695.
(Compare Nos. 9 and 14.)

14. GOTHIC WRITING. English, from the same source.
Note how the flourishes form a kind of middle tint, and decorate the page without obscuring the writing.

15. GOTHIC WRITING. English, from Multum in Parvo, or the Pen's Perfection by Edward Cocker, *c.* 1675.
The third word on the fourth line is meant for a contraction of Christian—but Cocker, or one of his predecessors, has evidently gone astray and mistaken the Greek ρ for a *p*.

16. GOTHIC WRITING. English, from Writing Improved by John Clark, 1714.

17. GOTHIC WRITING. German, from Kunst-richtige Vorshriften, Frankfort and Leipzig, 1702.
It is interesting to compare this late German example with the three English versions which precede it (Nos. 14, 15, 16), and to note how in this case the letters are all closed up and, as it were, flattened, whilst in the English work they are much rounder and more open.

18. GOTHIC WRITING by Peter Gery, 1670.
This shows a headline in large letters satisfactorily combined with smaller writing on the rest of the page.

19. A SMALL SCRIPT, rather Gothic in type, from the Exemplaria sive Formulae Scriptorae Ornatioris XXXIV of Houthusius, 1591. Note the character given to the writing by the long tails of the *s*'s.
(Compare Nos. 20 and 21.)

20. ANOTHER EXAMPLE of the use of the long *s*, from Poecilo-graphie by J. de Beaugrand, 1598.
Note the decorative value of the headline.
(Compare Nos. 19 and 21.)

21. GOTHIC WRITING, from the Spieghel Der Schrijfkonste by J. Van den Velde, 1605.
Note the characteristic long *s*'s and the curious form of the double *s*.
(Compare No. 26.)

22. CURRENT DUTCH WRITING, from the Tooneel der loflijcke Schrijfpen of Maria Strick, 1607.
(The four lines at the top of the page compare with Nos. 59 *et seq.*)

23. A PRETTILY SPACED RENDERING, in Gothic script, of a poem in three verses, from the same source.

24. CURRENT WRITING, to go with larger Gothic letters, from 'T Magazin oft' Pac-huys der Loffelijcker Penn-const by D. Roe-lands, 1616.

25. A MINUSCULE WRITING, showing certain affinities with Gothic. From the Paranimphe de l'Escriture Ronde of F. Desmoulins, 1625.
(Compare Nos. 19–23.)

26. ANOTHER CURRENT HAND with long tails to the *f*'s as well as the *s*'s, from 'T Magazin der Loffelijcker Penn-const by D. Roelands, 1616.

27. A CURIOUS and characteristic Dutch script, from the Exemplaar-Boek of A. Perlingh, 1679.

28. SECRETARY HAND, from A booke containing divers sortes of hands by J. de Beauchesne and John Baildon, 1571.

29. ANOTHER HAND showing the characteristic *d* of 28, from Chirographia by R. Gething, 1619.

30. AN EXAMPLE OF LETTRE PATTÉE, from the Exercitatio Alphabetica of C. Perret, 1569.

31. LETRA ANTIGUA. A kind of simple Roman letter with occasional flourishes introduced, which very much help the balance of the page. From the Recopilacion Subtilissima of J. de Yciar, 1548.

32. AN ITALIC HAND, in which some of the letters are adorned with flourishes. Spanish, from the Primera Parte Del Arte De escrivir by J. de Casanova, 1650.

33. A VERSION OF ROMAN MINUSCULE, having some affinity with the so-called "diplomatic hand." From the Libellus valde doctus elegans, utilis, multa varia scribendarum litterarum genera complectens of R. Wyss, 1549.

34. ROMAN SCRIPT, from the Exercitatio Alphabetica of C. Perret, 1569.

35. ROMAN SCRIPT, from Il Perfetto Scrittore of G. F. Cresci, 1569.

36. ROMAN SCRIPT, from the Primera Parte del Arte de Escrivir, by J. de Casanova, 1650.

37. ROMAN SCRIPT, from Kunst-richtige Vorschriften. Frankfort and Leipzig, 1702.

38. ITALIC WRITING, bearing some resemblance to No. 33. From the Anweissung einer gemeine handschrift, by J. Neudorffer the elder, 1538.

39. ITALIC WRITING, from the Exercitatio Alphabetica of C. Perret, 1569.

40.⎱CAPITALS AND SMALL LETTERS, from A booke contain-
41.⎰ ing divers sortes of hands by J. de Beauchesne and J. Baildon, 1571.

42. LETTERE PIACEVOLLE, a rather fantastic italic hand from the same source.
Note the unsatisfactory initial.

43. A VERY SIMPLE ITALIC HAND, from the Exemplaria sive Formulae Scripturae Ornatioris XXXIV. of J. Houthusius, 1591.

44.⎱TWO SIMPLE ITALIC HANDS, in which the tops of the *ll*'s
45.⎰ etc., show traces of the blob-like thickening which characterizes the more flowing hands illustrated in Nos. 53 to 64. From the same source as the preceding example.

46. SPANISH "BASTARDO" WRITING, from the Nueva Arte de Escribir of P. Diaz Morante, issued by Palomares in 1789.

47. REDONDILLO, or Spanish round hand, from the Arte de Escrevir of Francisco Lucas, 1580.
Note the curious form of the *d* which characterizes this type of writing.

48. BASTARDO Spanish Writing, from the same source.

49. SPANISH WRITING, from the Nueva Arte de Escribir of P. Diaz Morante, issued by Palomares in 1789.
Note the interesting treatment of the *p*'s and *q*'s.

50. ROUND HAND WRITING, from the Copy-Book of Richard Daniel, 1664.

51. ROUND HAND, by Peter Gery, 1670.

52. FRENCH AND BASTARD ALPHABETS, from L'Art d'Ecrire, by J.–B. Allais de Beaulieu, 1680.

53.⎫ EARLY EXAMPLES of the heavy endings to *l*'s, *d*'s, and other
54.⎭ letters with limbs above the line which form so conspicuous a feature in the next ten examples.   Italian, from the Libro di G.–B. Palatino, 1540.

55.⎫ MORE FORMED WRITING, Italian, from Il Perfetto Scrittore
56.⎭ of G. F. Cresci, 1570.

57. A BELGIAN RENDERING of the same characteristic, from the Exercitatio Alphabetica of C. Perret, 1569.

58. ANOTHER EXAMPLE of the same kind of writing, in which the Initial is less satisfactory and there is more tendency to introduce flourishes.   From the Exemplaria sive Formulae Scripturae Ornatioris XXXIV. of J. Houthusius, 1591.

59. A MORE RUNNING HAND, with the same characteristic blobs, from the Tooneel der loflijcke Schrijfpen of Maria Strick, 1607.

60. ANOTHER EXAMPLE, with typical penwork scrolls of the period above and below the writing.   From Les Oevres de Lucas Materot, 1608.

77. ANOTHER SLOPING WRITING, with flourishes, from Il Cancelliere of L. Curione, 1609. (Compare No. 61.)

78. RIOTOUS, but on the whole legible, flourish work. From 'T Magazin oft' Pac-huys der Loffelijcker Penn-const by David Roelands, 1616.

79. A WELL SET OUT piece of flourish writing, from Chirographia by R. Gething, c. 1619.

80.⎫ TWO EXAMPLES, in which the flourish is kept within bounds,
81.⎭ from the Poecilographie of J. de Beaugrand, 1633. Note the delicacy of the writing and the fanciful treatment of the initials.

82. RESTRAINED FLOURISH-WORK, from the same source.

83. SLOPING WRITING, with flourishes, from a book by Thomas Weston, 1681.

84. ANOTHER SLOPING HAND, with flourishes, from Kunstrichtige Vorschriften, 1702.

85. A SIMPLE CURRENT HAND, with a few flourishes added. From M. Baurenfeind's Vollkommene Wieder-Herstellung der Schreib-Kunst, 1716.

86.⎫ PORTUGUESE WRITING, with flourishes. From the Nova
87.⎭ Escola para aprender a . . . escrever by M. Andrade de Figueiredo, 1722.

88.⎫ CURRENT WRITINGS, from Chirographia by R. Gething,
89.⎭ c. 1619.

90.⎫ TWO WRITINGS WITH FLOURISHES, showing a deliber-
91.⎭ ately sought after effect where the ink has not run freely from the pen. From Richard Daniel's Copy-Book, 1664.

92. GREEK WRITING, from the same source.

93. GREEK WRITING, from The Universal Penman by George Bickham, 1743.

94. TYPICAL BORDER WORK, from the Tooneel der loflijcke Schrijfpen by Maria Strick, 1607.

PLATES

Joannes Oniseratione di
uina tituli San-
cti Joánis ante portam latina sancte
Romane ecclie pribr Cardinalis Archi-
episcopus Toletanus hispaniáru primas
ac Regnoz castelle maior chancellariz zc.

A.a.b.c.d.d.e.f.g.h.ij.k.l.m.m.n.n.η.
o.p.q.z.r.s.6.6.ss.st.v.u.x.y.z.z.z.z.

A.B.C.D.E.F.G.H.I.R.L.M.
N.O.P.Q.R.S.T.D.X.Y.Z.R.

ABCDEFGHIKLM
NOPQRSTVXYZ

Joannes de yciar Scribebat Cesaraugu
Ista Anno domini · 1 5 4 8 :~
J. D. V.

Iulius seruus seruorum Dei dilecto filio Vincentio de Andrea Canonico Suessan Salut et aplicam benedict Vite ac morum honestas aliaq; laudabilia probitatis et uirtutu merita super quibus apud nos fide digno commendaris testimonio :~ Crescus scrib.

Si quis aute hoc attemptare presumpserit indignationem omnipotentis Dei, ac beatorum Petri et pauli Aplorum eius se nouerit incursuruy. Dalt Rome : sanctum Petrum Anno incarnationis.

Joannes Franc Crescus Scri.

2, 3

Apostoles, y Euangelistas, y los setenta, y dos Disci-
pulos del Señor, los Santos Inocentes, y los Mart y-
res, los Pontifices, Confessores, y Doctores, los Sa-
cerdotes, Levitas, y Uirgenes te alaben eternamente,

The secretary hande.

It deserveth great chastisement that
with fearefull hardynes as a foole
determyneth hymself in high and difficult
thinges (with haftie conceit) whiche
requireth long determynation & aduise.

Het herte des rechtueerdigen, dichtet ðhat te antðhoorden is: daerentegen den mont der godloosen schuymet het boo= se. De heere is Verre Vanden godloosen: maer der recht= ueerdigen gebet Verhoort hy. Vriendelyck sien Verheucht het herte. Een goet geruchte maeckt Vet de gebeenten.

6

uijtneemendt vroom Capiteijn der Romeijnen, ðerdt vermaent door sijnen Soon dat hy soude Inneemen een Avantageuse plaetse met verlies van ðeijnigh volck: maer Fabius die niet sonder merckelijcke noodt sijne Soldaten en avon tuerde, antðoorde, ðilt gij een van die ðeijnige sijn.

7

c

reu, qui est Deritê, a defendu menterie, parquoy les menteurs sont
grandement a hayr. le Jeune homme qui s'accoustume a mentir,
il fait Dope & ouuerture a tous Dices, par lesquelz la Die est ma
culee & enlaidie tu Dois plus ouyr que parler, pource que tu ne
fcops iamais reprins quand tu te tais. Comme dit le Sage .

. a . b . c . d . e . f . g . h . i . h . l . m . n . o . p . q . r . s . t . u . x . y . z . z .

Like as the cutting of vines and other plants is cause of much better & more plentie of ȳ fruit: so the punishment of euill men, cause good men to flourish in a common welth.

M. Martin, Ang. scr.

mon admonnestoit les autres gens de rendre
leur Jeunesse le plus agreable par la Dettu, comme
estant l'unique ornement de cest âge: Et les
Dieux de n'adjoufter point a leur vieillesse la
laydeur du vice & Si Jozmite des mauvaises
mœurs, veu qu'elle a asses d'autres imperfections
a b c d e f f g h i k l m n o p q r z s s t u x y z et.

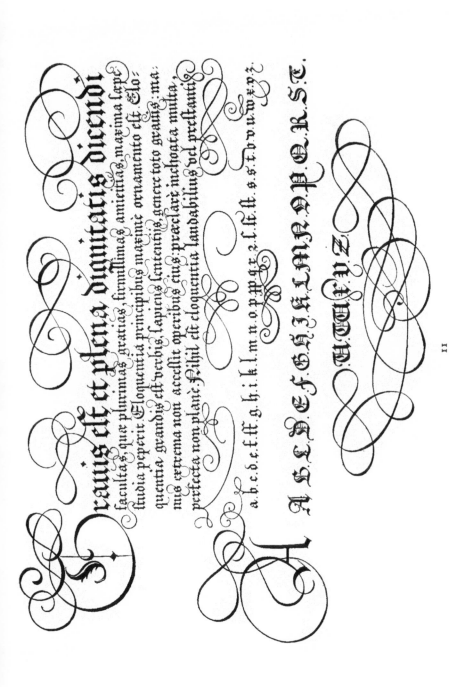

Gravis eſt et plena dignitatis dicendi facultas, quae plurimas gratias, firmiſſimas amicitias, maxima ſaepe ſtudia peperit. Eloquentia principibus maxime ornamento eſt. Eloquentiae grandis eſt verbis, ſapiens ſententiis, genere toto gravis; maximus extrema non acceſſit operibus eius: praeclare inchoata multa, perfecta non plane. Nihil eſt eloquentia laudabilius vel praeſtanti

a.b.c.d.e.ff.ſſ.g.h.i.k.l.m.n.o.p.qq.r.z.ſ.ſſ.ſt.ß.ſt.v.u.w.x.z.

A.B.C.D.E.F.G.H.I.J.K.L.M.N.O.P.Q.R.S.T.V.U.W.X.Y.Z.

alts mit jederman freundlich, vertraue aber unter
tausenden kaum einem. Vertraue keinem Freund,
du habst ihn denn erkannt in der Noht. Denn es
sind viel Freunde weil sie es genieſſen können, aber in
der Noht halten sie nicht Freund in der Noht, gehen 25. auf ein Loht. Solls ein harter Stand seyn.
So gehen ihr 50. auf ein Quintlein. Und ist man
cher Freund, der wird bald Feind, und wilſet er
nen, Mord auf ſich, er ſagets nach. Syrach im 6. Cap.

quod Nos de gratia nostra spetia-

liat ex certa Scientia et uero motu nostris Dedimus et Concess-

imus At per presentes pro nobis heredibus et Successoribus

nostris Damus et Concedimus Prefato B. M. omnia et

omnimoda Bona et Catalla et alia quaetunq; et quaegibi

ante hac tempora pettinebant Pardonauimus etiam eidem et

13

shall be a poor man. He that loveth wine and oil shall not be rich. Look not thou upon the wine when it is red when it giveth his colour in the cup when it moveth it self aright. At the last it biteth like a serpent, & stingeth like an add

14

Person who appropriates to himself the

Reputation that arises from anothers

Performance, discovers a barrenness of

Mind, a vainglorious humour, a lazy

Disposition, and an unjust Principle.

abcdefghijkllllmnopqrsstuvwxyz.

Der Mensch setzet ihm wohl für in seinem Herzen·
aber von Herrn kompt was die zunge reden
fol. Einem ieglichen dünckt seine Wege rein seyn·
aber alleine der Herr macht das hertz gewiß.
Befiehl dem Herren deine Wercke so werden deine
Anschläge fortgehen Der Herr machet alles umb
sein selbst willen auch den gottlosen zum bösen tag·

a b c d e ff g h i k ll m n o
p q r s ß st tt u v w y ß z

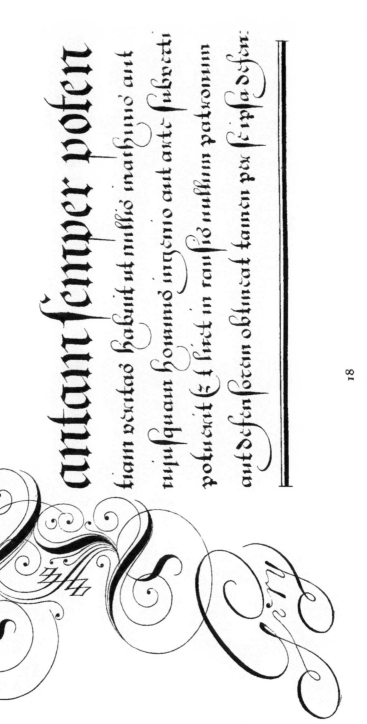

antan semper posen

tiam veritas habuit ut nullis matrimo aut

iniusquam hominis ingenio aut arte subiecti

potuerit (et licet in causis nullum patronum

aut defensorem obtineat tamen per se ipsa defen:

ourroucez vous dit le Prophete Et ne pechez point Et est a dire, moderez voltre ire, laquelle se pourroit conuertir en fureur, si par la victoire de soymesme elle n'estoit sur-montee. Ire empesche la pensee, trouble l'entendement, offense les Bons, irrite les mau-uais, et rompt a celuy qui la nourrist en soy. Il ne espargne personne condemne chascun, et Blaspheme les choses sainctes. Mettons luy donc en frain estroictement.

a. a. b. b. c. d. d. e. f. ff. g. b. b. i. k. l. m. n. o. p. p. q. r. 2. s. s. t. u. v. x. p. z.

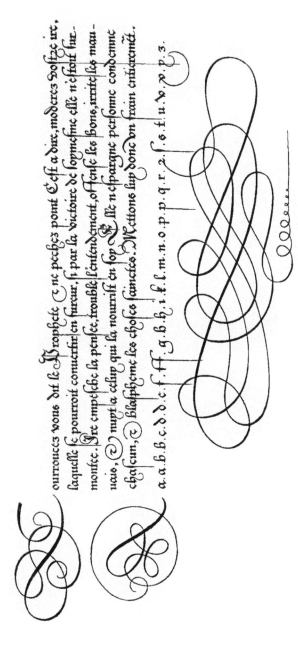

Eerde Wyse Hoochgeleerde ende seer Discrete Heeren,
Den Schouts, Borgemeesteren Schepenen ende
Raedt der Stadt Delff. Wy, Rect Maria Strick.

in perfecter gesontheyt. D'oorspoedige en langdurige Regieringe.

Mijne Heeren. Alsoo mt is doende dat wij begeerende
der Natur, silentum tuig, ... begeren
... spreken, ... als ... ... ende
dancke dit wel. ... Sijn de ... ziten, en ... onser
... ... Stellens ... ... wij ... ... mij niet
... vijffmaels ... ... tot ... dan mijn ... der tant
... tot ... ... te begrijpen ...
... onbegrijpelicken ... ... is dit ...
... maer ... tijt ... ... mijns ... ...
van der ... onderworpen ...

Datum Delff den 12. October
Anno 1606.

Dienste
Maria Strick

22

E

A Dieu, toute Gloire, en l'esingue.

ntendant on tresbonnoré et bien aimé Sire. Le desir qu'auez de sauoir comme j'ai profité a l'escriture, Ce m'a osé manquer pour ne paroir tre nonchalant a vous envoyer La presente, par laquelle pourrez voir ce qu'en ai appris partinsible mon avancement Grammatial et ma composition François, Espezant n'en encourir aucun reproche, a tant (apres m'estre recommande tres-humblement a vos bonnes graces) prie l'Eternel vous donner en santé longue et heureuse vie . ce 26 d'Avril Anno 1614

De tout vostre tres-obeissant Fils.

David . Roïlands .

24

Nous ne tenons pas Auiourd'huy q[ue] plusieurs iugeans.

Selon leurs sensualité & estans du tout ignorans de la vraye nature & immortalité de l'ame, on
constitue leur souuerain bien en la Volupté & iouissance des sens & plus les sens.
Aristippe & Epicures aultres qui s'attribuoyent faulsement le nom de Philosophe se sont efforcés par
plusieurs arguments & allegations pallian leurs malice de parolle graues & magnifiques, disan
Q[ue] nul ne pouuoit parfaictem[en]t acquerir la Volupté q[ue] ne fust vertueux, Mais ce q[ue] dit Cicero[n]
comme eux, peut leur seruir le Masque de leur imprudence soubs connaiss[an]ce de leur songie a scauoir
Q[ue] ne fault pas regarder seulement a ce q[ue] soyent les bonnes auec s'ill s'accorder a leur opinio[n]

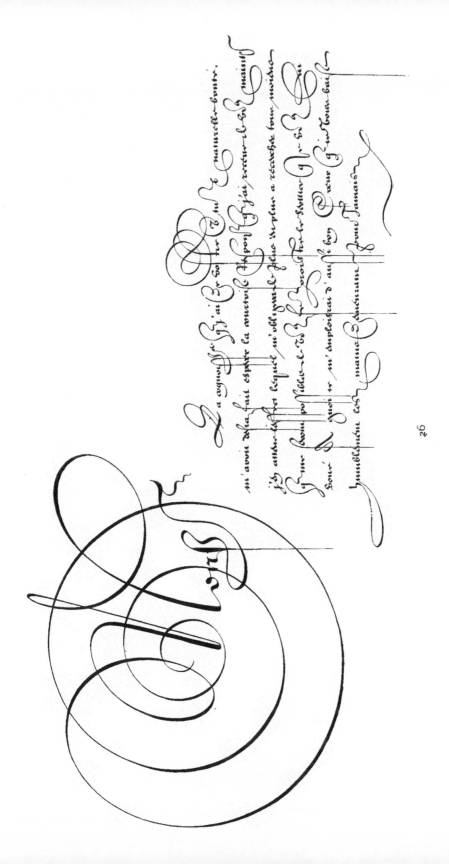

J'ay aussi receu la lettre que vous m'avez escripte...

Loys

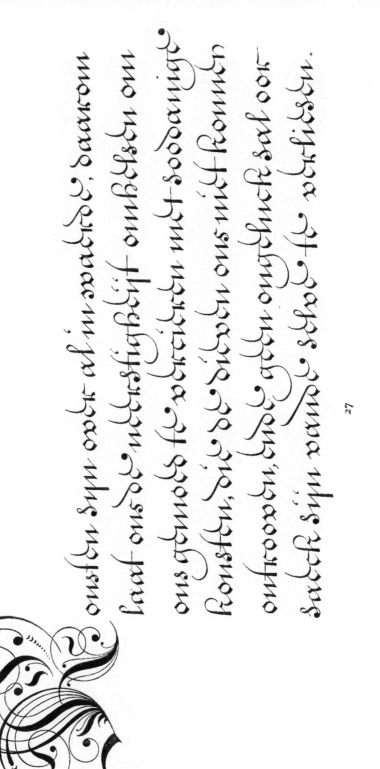

onsen syn ooer al in waare; daarom
laat ons de nedrstigheyt ombleen om
ons gemoeds te oeseren mit soodanyge
Ronsten, die de dieden ons mit Ronnen
ontrooden, eñ gen ongeluck sal oor
sulke syn raane; schoot te vrhiben.

27

Secretarie hande.

ene not that which is holy vnto dogge, neither cast ye
your pearles before swyne, least they treade them vnder
their feete. and the other turne agayne: and all to rent you
Axe and it shalbe genty yow. seke and ye shall fynd helpe

a b c d e f g h i k l m n o p q r s t u
v s t ff x y z.

28

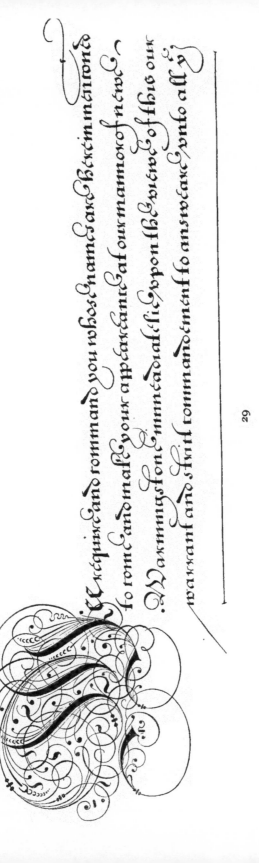

We require and command you whose name are Bextminstrones
to come and make your appearance at our mannor of newe
Waximngston ennence diatsili Vpon the sight of this our
warrant and strict commandement to answeare Vnto all y

aramaças encendidos Y espinas quemadas que reeman sobre el fuego se
pueden llamar las risas Y adulaciones del hombre loco. Y assi es vanidad
Y locura la alabança que viene de su boca. Por tanto es mejor oyr la
correcion Y amonestacion del hombre sabio Y prudente, que no las
canciones Y lisonjas de tales aduladores Y locos ./

a.b.c.d.e.f.g.h.i.k.l.m.n.o.p.q.r.f.ss.Gs.st.Gu.x.Y.y.z

30

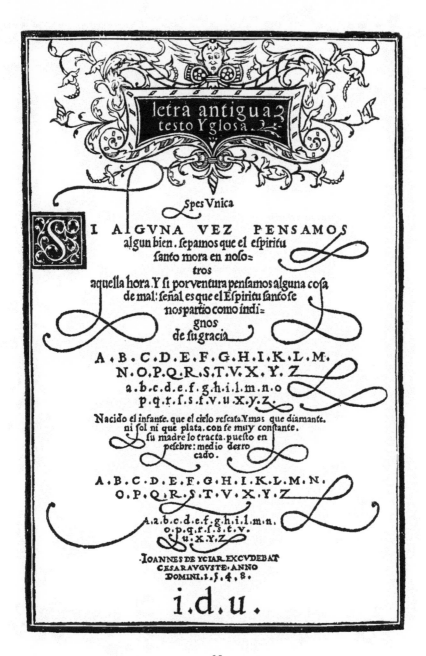

letra antigua
testo Yglosa

Spes Vnica

I ALGVNA VEZ PENSAMOS
algun bien. sepamos que el espiritu
santo mora en noso=
tros
aquella hora. Y si porventura pensamos alguna cosa
de mal: señal es que el Espiritu santose
nospartio como indi=
gnos
de su gracia

A.B.C.D.E.F.G.H.I.K.L.M.
N.O.P.Q.R.S.T.V.X.Y.Z
a.b.c.d.e.f.g.h.i.l.m.n.o
p.q.r.s.s.f.v.u.x.y.z.

Nacido el infante. que el cielo rescata.Y mas que diamante.
ni sol ni que plata. con se muy constante.
su madre lo tracta. puesto en
pesebre: medio derro
cado.

A.B.C.D.E.F.G.H.I.K.L.M.N.
O.P.Q.R.S.T.V.X.Y.Z

A.a.b.c.d.e.f.g.h.i.l.m.n.
o.p.q.r.s.s.t.v.
u.x.y.z.

IOANNES DE YCIAR EXCVDEBAT
CESARAVGVSTE ANNO
DOMINI.1.5.4.8.

i.d.u.

PRINCIPIO
PARA LOS PRIVILEGIOS QVE
SE ESCRIVEN EN PERGAMINO
EN LA SECRETARIA DE
LA CAMARA DE SV
MAGESTAD
El espacio desta quadricula se dexa en
blanco para el sello Real
En Madrid me escrivia Casanova

32

Nihil est amabilius uirtute, nihil quod magis alliciat homines ad diligendum. Quippe cum propter uirtutem & probitatem, etiam quos nunq̃ uidi, quodammodo diligimus. Cuius ea uis est, ut eam, quod maius est, in hoste etiam diligamus.

a b c d e ff fff ß h i k l m n o p q r ß s t u x y z.

Regiæ.Catholicæ.Maieſtatis.priuata
lege Bruxellis. Anno.Dom M.D.LXIX
die XIII.Febr.lata & firmata. *F de Langhe,*
ſub graui mulcta ſancitum eſt, ne quis
hoc Clementis Perreti opus imitetur, vel
quoquo modo imitatum toto proximo
ſexennio citra Chriſtophori Plantini
voluntatem diſtrahat ꝫꝫꝫꝫꝫꝫ

34

Domine Dominvs

noster quam admirabile
est nomen tuum in vniuersa
terra. Quoniam eleuata est ma=
gnificentia tua super cœlos ∴

Crescius scrib.

DOMINA MEA

Sancta Maria, me in tuam benedictam fidem, ac singulârem custôdiam & in finum misericordiæ tuæ, hódie, & quotidie. & in hora éxitus mei, & animam meam, & corpus meum tibi comméndo: omnem fpem meam & confolatiónem meam, omnes anguftias & miférias meas, vitam & finem vitæ meæ tibi committo; ut per tuam fanctiffimam intercefsiónem, & per tua merita, ómnia mea dirigántur, & difponántur ópera fecúndum tuam, tuique Filij voluntátem. Amen

Iustificati ergo ex fide pacem habeamus ad DEUM per Dominum nostrum IESUM CHRISTUM, per quem habemus accessum per fidem in gratiam istam, in qua stamus, & gloriamur in spe gloriæ filiorum DEI. Non solùm autem: sed et gloriamur in tribulationibus, scientes, quod tribulatio patientiam operatur, patientia autem probationem, probatio verò spem. Spes autem non confundit, quia Charitas DEI diffusa est in cordibus nostris, per Spiritum sanctum, qui datus est nobis. Ut quid enim CHRISTUS, cùm adhuc infirmi essemus, secundùm tempus pro impiis mortuus est?

P

aulus vinctus Christi Iesu. & Thimotheus frater. Philemon dilecto et adiutori nostro. & Apphiæ charissimæ & Archippo conmilitoni nostro. & ecclesiæ quæ in domo tua est. gratia vobis & pax a deo patre nostro. & domino Iesu Christo. Gratias ago deo meo semper, memoriam tui faciens in orationibus meis. audiens charitatem tuã & fidem quam habes in domino Iesu, & in omnes sanctos, ut communicatio fidei tuæ euidens fiat in agnitiõe omnis operis boni. in Christo Iesu. Gaudium enim magnum habui & consolationem in charitate tua quia viscera sanctorum requieuerunt per te frater. Propter quod multam fiduciã habens in Christo Iesu &c.

38

Rimuoui da te la prauità de la bocca, et la peruersità de la labra

discosta da te Gliocchi tuoi risguardino al dritto, et le palpebre

tue dirizzino auanti à te. Pondera la strada de piedi tuoi, et

Et tutte le vie tue siano Stabilite. Non declinare à la dextra,

ne à la sinestra, ma rimuoue el piede tuo dal male.

A. a. b. c. d. e. f. g. h. i. k. l. m. n. o. p. q. r. s. ff. t. u. v. x. y. z. &

CAPITALS.

A. A. A. A.
B. B. B. B.
C. C. C. c.
D. D. D.
E. E. E. E.
F. F. F. G.
G. G. H.
H. H. H.
I. f. f. f.
I. K. K. K.
L. L. L. L.
M. M. M.
N. N. N.
O. o. O.
P. P. P. P.
Q. Q. Q. Q.
R. R. R. R.
S. S. S. S. T. T. T.
V. v. v. v.
W. W. x. x. x.
Y. Y. Y. Y.

Small Lettres

a b c d e f g h i k l m n o p g q r ſ s
t u v w x y z z & & &

a b c d e f g h i k l m n o p q . ſ s t .
v u w x y z z & &

a b c d e f g h i k l m n o p l r ſ s t .
v w u v x y z & & & &

Lettres doubles, & tyes

æ. œ ff ff ſſ ſſ ij ij z ll m mm rr ſl ſs tt w.

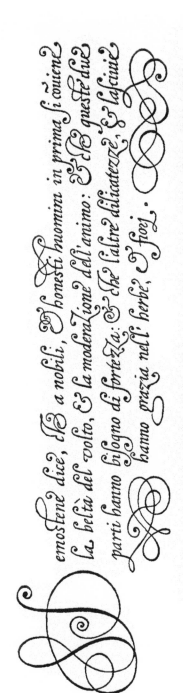

Lettere Piaceuole.

emostene dice, Che a nobili, Ch'honesti huomini in prima si couiene la beltà del volto, Et la moderazione dell'animo: Che queste due parti hanno bisogno di fortezza: Che l'altre dilicatezze, Et alcune hanno grazia nell'herbe, Et fiori.

A B C D E F G H I L M N O P Q R S T.

EPIGRAMMA

Dmisso ingemuit Perreto Belgica Pubes :
Artem morte Viri questa perire simul.
Hactenus : et merito. sed iam sedabitur ille
(Ad Calamum, HOVTHVSI, te præeunte) dolor.
Tu damna hæc pensas Tabulis, queis mille recludit
Scribendi Veneres ingeniosa manus.
Quid? pensas dixi? longe immò clarior isthoc
Ævo Chartæolis Victor es in Stadijs.

Nam quis non stupeat, pulchræ modò qui artis amator,
Egregium hoc Pennæ luxuriantis Opus?
Crede mihi, a te Vno posthac pendere Juuentus
Eliget, & ductus non nisi amare tuos.
Sed scin quæ maneat te, HOVTHVSI, gratia facti,
Præmia quæ et dextræ penupotenitis erunt?
Nempe hæc: Terrarum duersas Penna per oris
Impete pernici te vehet Artificem.

Ger. Subernius van Corck.

Il ne fault pas porter impatiemment ce que l'on ne ſçauoit vaincre par force, ne par conſeil, comme la mort & autres choſes. Mais il conuient eſtimer qu'il ne nous aduient choſes nouuelle, qui ſoit contre la condition de tous mortelz. Que nous ſçet il doncques de lamenter & plorer ſinon, que nous ſommes vous plus legers & inconſtant. Se Sage donne auſſi ce remede contre les voices.

L. a.b.c.d.e.f.g.h.i.i.k.l.m.m.n.n.o.o.p.p.q.r.z.z.ſ.s.ß.t.u.vu.x.x.y.y.z.z.

44

Si ton amy t'a fasché en quelque chose, en quoy tu n'es pas grandement offence, tu le dois porter de bon cueur. Il y a des gens que pour la moindre faute du monde n'ont point de honte de rompre une grande & longue amitie mais ilz ne font pas parfaictz amys, car le vray amy supporte l'impefection de son amy, & en enduze usques au bout ————

a.b.c.d.e.f.g.h.h.i.y.k.l.m.m.n.n.o.o.p.|p.q.r.z.f.s.ß.ſt.v.u.u.x.x.y.y.z.

Calografia enseña à dibuxar, delinear, ò sea escribir con ayre gallar=
día y perfeccion las letras grandes y pequeñas de nuestro abecedario,
siguiendo el caracter y buen gusto de los famosos pendolistas, de
modo que quando se escribe con caracteres bastardos, no se dẽ los Can-
cellarescos, ò al contrario, porque cada especie de letra, por exemplo la
Romanilla, Grifa. &c. tienen sus abecedarios con cierta figura y
delineacion accidental con que se diferencian unos de otros.

-:·Redondillo:-

Enel campo me meti,
aliuiar con mi desseo,
comigo mismo peleo
defiendame Dios demi
Si yo mismo me doy

-·: guerra, y :-

A a b c d e f f g h z i j l l m
n o p q r z s t v u x y y z z
Æ. Frañ, lucas. Año 1570

BASTARDO

O clementissimo y benignissimo
Jesu enseñame, endereçame, ya
yudame señor en todo. O muy
dulcissimo Jesu quando tu visi-
tares mi coraçon alegrarse han
todas mis entrañas. Tu eres mi
gloria y alegria de mi coraçon:
tu eres mi esperança y mi refrigerio enel dia de mi tribulaciõ,
y trabajo.

Frañ, Lucas lo escreuia. Año
M. D LXXVI.

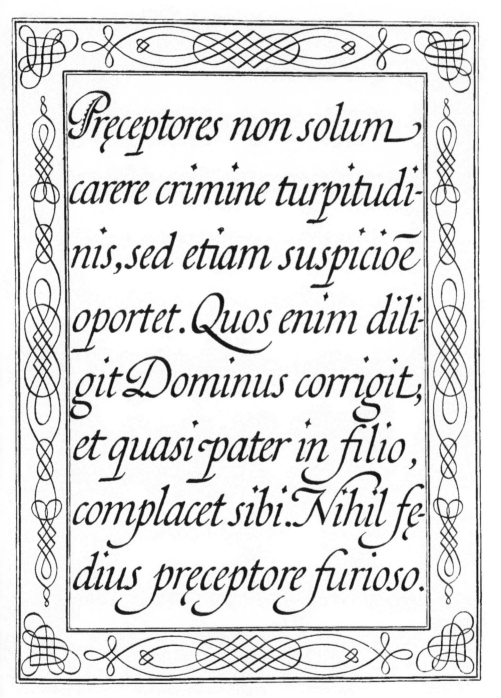

Preceptores non solum carere crimine turpitudinis, sed etiam suspicioē oportet. Quos enim diligit Dominus corrigit, et quasi pater in filio, complacet sibi. Nihil fedius preceptore furioso.

Eternitie is the
entire and perfect Possession of a Life: togea=
ther and att once that nevr shall have end
But how can that be difined which hath no
Limit. It is a Circle running back into it self;
whose Circumference is without end .

Knowledge is the treasure of the Minde but Discretion is the Keye without which it lyes dead in the dulnesse of a fruitlesse rest The practique part of Wisdome is the best There is a loving noblenesse some are graced with farre transcending the motions of a timed studie

a a, b ib, c c, ∂ ∂ ∂e, e e,

fi, ff ff, g gg, hh, i jÿ, C Œ

ui uui, u ŋŋ, o v pp, q g, r vr

ʃ ʃʃa, t tt L, u v uu, x xx,

y v, z z x eu.

a a, b ib, c, ∂ d ∂, e i e, ff ff,

g gg, h ib h, i j, l il L, m mm,

n nn o v, p p, q g g, r z rz, s

sʃa t tt L, u v v, x x x y x y

z z, et et et eu.

De' sopradetti tre Tratti, siano false, ò
uero imaginatiue, & non
cauate dalla esperientia
geometricamente;
per
esser'impossibile misurare
effettualmente vna cosa si piccola, hò
Voluto aprire il modo ritrouato da me,
co'l quale hò uisto chiara
mente esser
cosi.
Et però, uolendo uenire alla prat
tica, e uedere per esperien
tia le sopradette misure,
potrete pigliare
(na)

Benche in parlamento non uengon mai
accompagnate' cò quelle' sopradett'
che' hanno il punto
di sotto.

℃ La distantia de l'una lettera à l'altra de
ui' esser' quáto è lo spatio fra le' due' gã
be' del. n.

ꟲusa mihi causas memora ꝛc̄ʃ

℃ La distantia dall'una parola à l'altra'
ha da esser' tanto, che' ui entri un
.ò. in Questo modo.

ꟲ irtuti°fortuna°comes.

℃ La distantia dall'un uerso à l'altro deue'
esser' (quanto alla uera ragione') lo
spatio di doi corpi, (come' uedete'.

54

Omnipotens sempiterne Deus, fundamentum om=
nium virtutum amator, et conseruator omnium in
te sperantium, pijssime consolator omnium ad te cla=
mantium qui cęlum et terram de nihilo fecisti vni=
uersum mundum pugillo conclusisti naturam hu =
manam mirabiliter vnitiue assumpsisti, & q Cresci?

In nome di Christo noi siamo illuminati, perche Lui 3
e la vera Luce del mondo, che illumina ogni huomo che
uiene al mondo, come disse. ego sum lux mundi. Et 3
San Giouanni dicea. Erat lux uera quæ illuminat
omnem hominem venientem & q
Crescius Scribebat.

55, 56

I

Quel egli bile esser la bona fama, et le molte richeze et bona qua-
tia, più et aggento et oro, Aruede et il savero si contrano: il fattore
de tutti loro, e il Signore. castuto prevede il male, et se asconde: ma
gli sciocchi trapassano recevendo danno Per humilita et timore
del Signore, vengono richezze gloria, et vita. Sine labore nihil.

.a.b.c.d.e.f.g.h.k.l.m.n.o.v.p.p.q.r.r.f.s.st.v.u.x.y.z.&.

pres l'honneur de Dieu, la reuerence de tes parens t'est commandee tant
par la loy diuine, que par tous les Sages, laquelle reuerence ne gist pas
seulement en honneur exterieur, ains aussi en amiablete. Beneuolence,
seruice, & asistence. Ce commandement doit estre soigneusement
persuade aux ieunes enfans, afin qu'ilz le gardent, come tesmoigne S.P.

a. a. b. c. d. e. f. g. h. i. k. l. m. n. o. p. q. r. s. s̄ t. t. u. v. x. x. y. z

ROBERT Roy de Sicile disoit
en iour qu'il aimoit mieux les Livres que sa
couronne, et qu'il avoit plus cher la doctrine
et science par luy acquise en la Lecture des bon..
nes Lettres.que Les honneurs et richesses de son
Royaume.

Marie Stric..

Tous les plus grands biens du monde sont parsemez d'ennuits et de sollicitudes
et n'y a condition en la vie humaine plus redoutable que la prospere. Pour garantir
nostre felicité nous auons besoin d'vne autre felicité, et pour les souhaits acomplis il
faut trese d'autres souhaits. Car tout ce qui auuent pour le regard de ceste vie pend à vn
filet. Nul ne prend plaisir aux choses qui douent tomber. Donc tres-miserables
sont ceux qui amassent auec trauail ce qu'ilz ne peuuent garder auec grand soing

Alla Regina del Cielo

Beatissima Vergine vnico refrigerio nell'amarissime mie tempeste a te'
muolgo ogni speranza come a tranquillissimo, e lieto porto oue l'anima
mia desidera di finire il periglioso camino di questa mondana vita sup=
plicandoti, ese con l'auea del tuo diuino auto vogli secondare questa mia
fatica insino all'vltimo fine a laude e gloria del tuo santissimo nome Amen.

Lodouico Curione Scriueua in Roma

The honor due vnto parents, is none otherwise to bee vn=
derstanded but to iudge commendable, reverentlie, &
honorablie of our parents; and to esteeme well of all
theire doings. not onelie as of elders. but principally.
because they bee parents whom god vsed as instrumets
to bring vs to this transitorie beeing which we haue

To Dames of Acref

Avoir du Seigneur Dieu la crainte et connoissance.

Est le but principal de toute sapience. A. A.

Bien qu'on homme ayt acquis des biens en abondance,

Pauvre il sera tous jours s'il n'a pas suffisance. B.

Mesme corps fut iadis nostre verd, puis meusseau

Naguere Champignon, et maintenant oiseau. M. M.

Naõ admitem as sciencias, aquem com desejos a ellas senaõ applica; porque mal se compadecem empenhos do entendimento com distrahimentos da vontade.

Ainda q̃ hum homem seja senhor do mundo, se onaõ for dos seus appetites podese contar entre onumero dos infelices, porque do descanço do espirito depende afelicidade da vida.

Andrade

K

Iserere mei Deus secundum magnam misericordi-
am tuam: Et secundum multitudinem miserationum
tuarum dele iniquitatem meam. Amplius lava me ab
iniquitate mea: & à peccato meo munda me. Quoniam iniquitatem meam ego cognosco: & peccatum meum
contra me est semper. Tibi soli peccavi & malum
coram te feci. Ut justificeris in sermonibus tuis, &
vincas cum judicaris. Ecce enim in iniquitatibus.

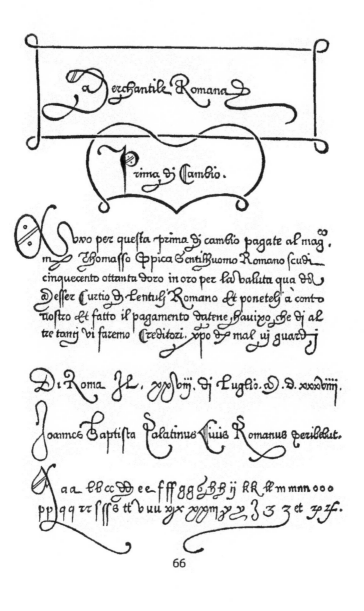

La Merchantile Romana

Prima di Cambio.

Uvo per questa prima di cambio pagate al mag.co
m. Thomasso Oppica Gentilhuomo Romano scudi
cinquecento ottanta d'oro in oro per la baluta qua
Desser Curtio di Lentuli Romano et ponetela à conto
nostro et fatto il pagamento datene Hauiso che di al
tre tanti vi faremo Creditori. xpo di mal vi guardi

Di Roma HL. xxbiij. di Luglio. D. D. xxxbiij.

Joannes Baptista Palatinus Ciuis Romanus scribebat.

A aa bb cc dd ee fff gg hh ij kk ll m mnn ooo
pp qq rr sss tt v uu xx xxyy y z zz z et zf.

Merchantile Milanese;

Quel poco che occorre dire sopra le lettere Merchantij
(Conciosia che si imparino piu p̃ pratica che p̃ regola)
è questo; che tutte quelle che han corpo, nascono dal
quadro perfetto. Et la penna vuol esser teprata, tonda
senza cantoni, et nõ ciotta; per che questa lettera vuol
tondeggiare et esser dritta, senza dependẽtia alcuna; Et
la varieta che si vede da l'una Merchantile à l'altra;
consiste solamẽt̃ ne le haste, et ne' tratti; eccetto la Ge-
nouese, che baria queste due lettere. e. et. r. come si
uede per gli loro Alphabet   :~

Principij onde si formano le lettere,

∿c o a a ⌐ℓ ℓ -c c -d d ∂∂ -c e ∫ ʃ ʃ -c g δ ⌐ℓ ℓ ij ⌐ℓ ℓ
ℋ -r m r n -o ∫r ͡p -c q -⌐z z ∫ ℓℓ ℓʃ lt tt vu r v
∿v x ☉ ∿v y ↄʒ ʒʒ -ʒp :

Tutte le soprascritte lettere si fanno ad un sol tratto ∂
pẽna, Eccetto queste, f, p, t, che si fanno in doj, Et que
sta vna sola f, in ₰

A. a. b. b. c. d. d. d. Lettera Mercbantie. e. e. fif. f. f. b. b. b. b. y.

Carlo dj Bartolomeo Altrobrandj et Lorenzo Malegonelle et Compagni
Di Lione ston dare gz di xxbiij di Ottobre per la natura di tanti deappi ba=
unj gz di detto p somma et quantita, j pno noueceni 96 di Camera
egli dinarj sono da pagarsj ptutt el sopradir Come in gz appare per lj
ricordj nel Et piu deno dare gz 16 p somma, et quantita, dun
promessa fatta gz dui Quarto 96 di camera, egli sono p la natura
j fanti fanuj monaghinj frauuti gz di 16 eh eglj sono da pagarsj traf

A. l. l. k. m. n. o. p. Instructione Mercare. q. q. r. f. ff. s. t. u. x. y z.

68

Alcuno à diuentar buono non incomincia, se a La
sciare il male non si dispone. Parimente, chiunqz
vuole ascendere La scala, prima il piede Leua da
La terra: cosi nella diuina scuola nõ si puo dare
principio al bene, se non col prima togliere
al male 👁. Crescius scribebat.

Ogni Suomo, che opera male ha in odio La
Luce, et non viene alla luce accioche, L'ope
sue maligne non siens manifeste et riprese.
Ma colui che segue La verità viene alla
Luce accioche, L'ope sue suens chiare pche le
sons fatte in Dio. Crescius scribebat

D. D. Francisco Lansbergio Vigilan-
tissimo apud Roterodamos Verbi
Administro.

Plurima Pierides referunt tibi præmia Musæ,
Qui non Pæonia tantum præcellis in arte,
Sed quod maius opus, tu afflatus Numinis aura
Ætherei, errores animi, scelerumque salebras,
Quodque tenebrarum est in cæco pectore lustras;
Ostendens populis, quæ sit via certa Salutis.
Macte istis Francisce bonis, vestigia Scisti
Sic preme, dum corpus curas, animumque serenas.

Tuus. Velduis.

71

Ad Doctss. Clariss.mumq̄ Dñum Dñu Petrum
Carpenterum Scholæ Rotterodamensis Rectore
Vigilantiss.mum.

Non levis ēt operæ moveran fræna Iuventæ,
Adque Aganippæi ducere fontis aquas.
Sentit qui ludi maculatur pulvere, sentit
Inter curratos qui tonat ore choros.
Hoc, Carpenteri, nec tantum hoc optime præstas,
Dum nullum frustra tempus abire sinis.
O te felicem cerebri! tibi scriber ludus
Quodque opus ēt aliis hoc tibi præter opus.

72

L: Prudentis de Prosoops

gevraecht werdt, waeromm by sulcken eenstigen

straffer was van zyne discipulen soo seyt hy ge-

antwoort. Die middernin doen docs ooc alzoo

mtt de patienten daer mede te leeren gewinnet dat

zy die lasteren ende gebreken straffe ende nz de mensce

Maria Strick

L

Monsieur Guillaume Sylvius Recteur
des Garnisons de Heusden.

Mons. Sylvius, Suis que je n'ignore pas de quel zele vous aymez
la langue Francoise delaquelle jadis avez faict profission et quel rang
d'honneur tient en vous la tresnoble science de bien escrire. Certes jen
ne pourrois sans perdant l'honneur que l'on vous en doibt) vous passer
tacitement Parquoy vous prie d'accepter ce petit exemplaire pour sommage.
vous ou suis fia

Datum Delff le 12. de May
An. 1606.

Escris bien affectionne

Maria Strick

Recomonnette donc q'avant toutes choses
on face Requestes Prieres Suplications trac tions
de graces pour tous Hommes: Sp. les Rois,
pour tous ceux q. sont Constitués en Dignité,
afin q. nous puissions mener vie paisible et
tranquille en toute pieté et Honnesteté.

facile à imiter pour les femmes.

Nous deuons peser et estimer les biens et faueurs que nous receuons de

Dieu, auec nos biens temporels, beaucoup plus que tous les maux qui

nous sçauroient aduenir.

Entre les anciens la pauureté ne pouuoit empescher vn homme d'estre iuste, sage, et vaillant,

et s'abusent ceux qui estiment que sans grands moyens vn homme puisse faire acte vertueux

comme si la vertu procedoit de richesse, et le vice de pauurcté.

aaa bbb ccc ddd eee fff ggg hh ii ll mm nn oo pp qq rr ss ſſ tt vv uu xx yy zz

All Ill.re et molto Mag.co Sig.r Lelio Foresieri

Io so ch(e) V.S. Ill.ma è così compita di gentilezza et di nobilissimi costumi quanto sia di dottrina, et d'ogni altra bellissima virtu et ch'e non potro in quesi pochi versi stendeomi secondo il desiderio mio nelle sue pregiate qualità ma gradisca al presente la seruitù, et oseruanza mia diuotissima a'menti suoi, et in= suome il carattere che tanto le piace et ch'ella souene così bene. Et io bacio le mani di V.S. Ill.ma Sig.r Lodouico Curione scriueua in Roma

Uno de gl'amici d'Alessandro
gli domandò qualche quantità di danari, & (Aristace alcun)
sue figliuole, a cui fe' dar subito più di Cinquanta talenti, qual
era grandissima somma, allhora disse, Porrillo, dicci talenti ò
Signore, eranno assai. Rispose Alessandro, assai
certo era à te il riceuere, ma non assai à me il dare.

CAROLUS DEI GRATIA.

Magnæ Brittanniæ Franciæ et Hiberniæ Rex fidei defensor

Serenissimus atque Illustrissimus Principibus, Ducibus,

Comitibus, Thalassiarchis, Strategis, Urbium, Portuum, Viarii

Portuum, Fluminum, Præfectis Omnibus, et singulis Archi-

Episcopis, Episcopis, et Magistratibus quibuscunque, Salutem.

Quibas nostras ad vos perfert litteras Nobilissimus et Honora-

tissimus Dominus Carnettus Demetrius natione Græcus,

pro vt ex varijs testimonijs fide dignis certo accepimus exc Achaia

Peloponeso præclaris maioribus est oriundus, Quæcumin &c.

Stratonicus se mocquoit anciennement de la grande superfluité des Rhodiens, disant qu'ils batissoient comme s'ils eussent esté immortels, et se ruoient en cuisine côme s'ils eussent eu bien peu de temps a viure. Mais les audacieux acquieroient comme magnifiques, et dependoient côme mecaniq̃ ressemblans aucunem̃t aus mulets qui portent sur le dos des charges d'or et d'argent et ne mangent que du foin. Et comble de leur misere est que pô accroistre et conseruer leur cheuance ils ne se soucient de la justice.

Aa bb cc dd ee ff ſſ gg hh y iſ ll mſ ll mm nn oo pp ee qq g ꝫ rr ſſ ſſ tt vu uu xx yy zz

Vous estre acquis le los d'vn Hercule indontable
De lauriers dés enfance auoir le front semé,
Par clemence & douceur estre des bons aimé,
Vous rendre par justice aux meschans redoutable.
En vos serments jurez vous monstrer veritable,
Vous voir Pere du peuple à bon droict estimé,
Auoir releué seul vostre Estat opprime,
Lors que tous presageoient sa cheute ineuitable.
SIRE, ces faicts sont grands, & tres-dignes de vous,
ROY. le plus grand des Roys, que vous surpassez tous.
Mais quand vostre bonté d'une aureille abaissee
Entend des plus petits la suppliante voix,
Vostre grandeur par vous est autant surpassee,
Comme vous surmontez en grandeur tous les Roys.

81

M

SOCRATES estant mandé du Roy Archelaüs, à fin q'il fallast trouuer, luy promettant de grands tresors. Il luy manda que la mesure de farine se vendoit en Athenes vn double, & que l'eau n'y coustoit rien. Par ainsi encores q'il semble que je n'aye pas beaucoup de biens si en ay-je assez puis-que je men contente. Aussi disoit Menandre, Pain pou manger & eau pour boire en somme, Sont seulem necesse a l'home. La suffisance et mediocrité sont au lieu de grande cheuance, et cause de la tranquillité d'esprit.

De Beaugrand

TO THE READER

BEING neither Master nor Professor of Writing, I may be Censur'd as an impertinent Intruder into an other mans Province, by Publishing these my unpolished Essayes. I did not purpose, at first, either a Book, or a Publication: but have been prevail'd with therein beyond my primitive intention. As I have had Diversion & Delight in composing, if any one shall receive Pleasure, or Profit, in perusing, or imitating these imperfect Ideas, it will afford a Satisfaction Beyond imagination to the Author of y^m

Regnum cœlorum, regnum felicissimum, regnum carens morte & vacans fine, cui nulla tempora succedunt per ævum, ubi continuus sine nocte dies, nescit habere tempus, ubi victor miles post laborem Donus ineffabili-bus cumulatur, nobile perpetua caput amplectente corona Utinam remissa peccatorum mole, me ultimum servorum CHRISTI jusserit divina pietas hanc carnis sarcinam deponere, ut in sua civitatis gaudia æterna repausandus transirem, sanctissimis supernorum choris intereßem, cum beatissimis spiritibus gloriæ conditoris asisterem

A B C D E F G H I K L M N O P Q R S T V W X Y Z. ETC:

A

Antiochus in venatione quadam, dum foras infectatur, ab amicis et famulis aberrat, casamque hominum egenorum iis ignotus intravit. Cum autem inter cœnandum regis mentionem fecisset, responsum est ille, Regem alioquin ternuum esse, sed eum plerasque negotia amicis improbis committere, plurima negligere, sæpeque res necessarias omittere, quod venationis nimium studiosus esset. Ac tunc quidem tacuit, sed postero die, cum prima luce satellites ad casam venirent, et allata purpura ac diademate agnosceretur, Ab eo, inquit, die, quo vos mihi adiunxi, heri primum veros de me sermones audivi. Vtinam eodem modo et alii Principes de his vitiis, quæ in plerisq aulis nimis usitata sunt, sæpe admonitiones audirent et laudatissimi regis Antiochi exemplum imitantes, ea clementer agnoscerent, et emendarent.

A a a b b c c d d e e f f f g g g h h i i k k l l l l m m m n n n n o v p p g g r r r ſſ ſſ ſ s
t tt v v u u w w r x y ỹ z z z.

Se ver com os olhos corpo=
raes o artificio, e fermosura das cre=
atueas, e os Metaes, e pedras preciosas
compostas de terra causaõ tanta a=
legria á vista do coraçaõ humano;
que alegria, e contentamento será ver
a fermosura dos Anjos, e Bemaven=
tueados, e a infinita belleza do Mes=
mo Deos.
Se de ouvir o som, e musica da voz hu=
mana, e harmonia dos insteumentos,
se recebe tanta suavidade que fica o
homem suspenso, e perde o sono, e comi=
da por este gosto; que suavidade será
ouvir com os ouvidos da alma os can=
tos, e melodias, comque os Anjos
Louvaõ, e glorificaõ a Deos.

Na gravidade, e valentia do geſto, com que o Artifice comproem a imagem lhe infunde o reſpeito. O retrato de hum Prĩcipe naõ se inculca ſómente pela eminencia da Coroa, tambem se dà a conhecer pela soberania da Magestade. O venerável aspecto, e decente gravidade andaõ anexos às mayores virtudes: ou para se inculcarem regias, ou para se divizarem soberanas: De pouco importa a fidalguia do lenho para os agrados da vontade, se desmerece pelo feitio, o que outro mais inferior avulta pela imagem. Andre

uirtus Pompeius sexti filius, multis et uetoribus causis necessitudinis mihi coniunctus est. Is cum antea meis commendationibus et rem et gratiam, et autoritatem suam tueri consueuit: nunc profecto te prouintia obtinente meis literis assequi debet, ut neminem intelligat commendatiorem umquam fuisse. quamobre a te maiorem in modum peto, ut cum omnes meas neque artius obseruare pro nostra necessitudine debeas. hunc in primis ita in tuam fidem recipias, ut ipse intelligas nullam rem sibi maiori uini, aut ornamento quam meam commendationem esse potuisse. Vale

Gething

plants and other creatures, haue their growth and mortalls to a period, and then their declinacion and decay; except onlie the Crocodile, who euer grow'th bigger and greater, euen till death. Soe haue all passions and perturbacons of mans minde, their intencons and remissions, increase, and decrease; except onlie malicious Reuenge, for this, the longer it lasteth, the stronger it waxeth.

Jehoua es mi Pastor
no me faltara: En lugares
De yerua me hara yazer: junto
a aguas de reposo me pastoreara
hara boluer mi alma. guiarmesa
por sendas de Justicia Por
Su Nombre

Spem locat in Te Domine,
Qui novit Tua quod finis
Vis careat, Nomen adorat
pijs Precibus honorat
Ergo novum ferte melos
Regi, Qui manibus Coelos

E mare, terramq, creavit
Bonis undique decoravit
Qui miserator, miserum
oblivifcitur haud, verum
Sanguipetas perdit atroces,
Eveniem Juvat ope voces

Mitior ô adspice me, Hostilesq, dolos deme,
frange minas perde tumentes Cruento facinore gentes.
Gloria Patri Superum Cunctarum Domino rerum

Hostis Jo jam Capitur, Passis retibus ambitur,
Ipse suâ fallitur Arte, jacens perfola vaga marte
Unigena gratia Nato, Decus Pneumatiq3 Sacrato.

ΔΕΚΑ ΛΟΓΟΣ.

Οὐδὲ θεοῖσι Θεῷ ἰδίῳ σὺν προσκύνει ἄλλοις.   α

Ἄπνοον οὐ κόσμῳ ποιήσεις παντὸς ἄγαλμα.   ϛ

Μήποτε μὲν μελέως περιλάμβανε τὔνομα θεῖο.   γ

Ἑβδομάνη θήσεις καλὰ παντοῖς παῦε πόνοισι.   δ

Ἄχρι ὀφειλομένω γονέας καὶ ἅζε καθήκω.   ε

Οὐδένα ἄνθρωπον θανάτῳ δολοέντι φονεύσῃς.   ζ

Σύζυγον ἠδ' ἑτέρα λέκτρον καὶ μηδὲ βέβηλο.   η

Κλέμματα μὴ πράξεις· παλάμας ἀπὸ παντὸς ἐπίσχης. θ

Προσκαλῇ εἰ μάρτυρ μάρτυρ μὴ ψεῦδος ἔσσο.   ι

Γείτονος οὔτι μάοις μήπως θεράποντα γαμήλην. κ

Ἴσθι πιστεύων τὸν κόσμον εἶναι φθαρτόν, ὅπη καὶ γέγονε μετ' δὲ τὴν φθορὰν, εἰς ἀφθαρσίαν πάλιν μεταποιούμενον. οὐδὲν γὰρ τῶν παρὰ Θεοῦ γεγονότων εἰς ὃ μὴ ὂν χωρήσει, κἂν ὃ τῆς ἁμαρτίας προάπτωμα, ἅμα ἡμῖν, καὶ πᾶσαν τὴν κτίσιν τῇ διαλύσει συγκατεδίκασεν.

TOONEEL.

Der loflijcke Schrijfpen

en dient te wande doud
hemmen dr jeucht int
lucht gebracht door;

MARIA STRICK

Franloyfche School-houdinne binnen do Coninrl vermaerdr
Stadt Delff Gesneden Door Hans Strick Ano 1607

enon dit . que ceux la qui ont le desir de
vertu enracine en Leurs cueurs . soudain
se mettent en devoir de cercher le moyen
principal pour y attaindre . qui est le
scavoir des bonnes Lettres : que (comme
dit un autre Philosophe) ie ne scay s'il
y a rien de plaisant au monde oultre
icelles .

uand nous faisons du bien aux indigens.

Et aux amis que languer deconforte. Nous ne

devons loublier aux gens. Mais tant que tost.

La memoire en fort morte. Au mamcmdem mcm

bminrm sn gm em bnnor mu em gm mr m vr rr z.

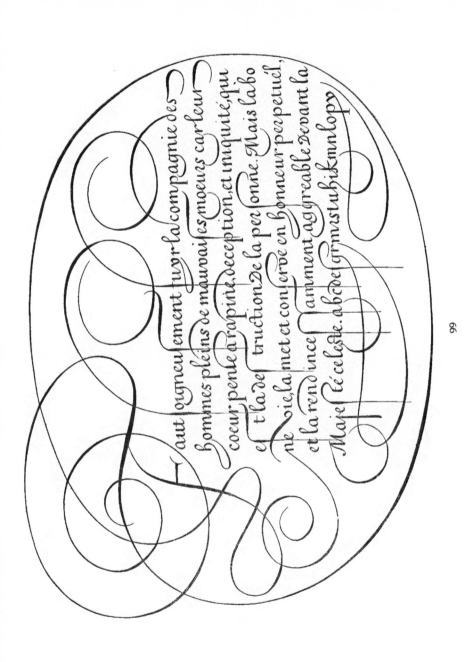

...aut soigneusement suyr la compagnie des
hommes pleins de mauvaises moeurs car leur
coeur pente à rapine, deception, et iniquité, qui
et la destruction de la personne. Mais la bo
ne vie, la met et conserve en bonheur perpetuel,
et la rend ince samment agreable devant la
Majesté celeste. abcdefgrmstubikmnlopx

Lucius Brutus Eques Romanus adolescens omnibus rebus ornatus in meis familiarissimis est meque observat diligentissime cuius cum patre magna mihi fuit amicitia iam inde a quaestura mea Siciliensi. Omnino nunc ipse Brutus Romae mecum est sed tamen domum suum suis et rem familiarem et procuratores tibi sic commendo.

n vieux Maistrô
dit quand L'aijde
du Humain manqz
alors vient L'aijde Divine

Een Oud Meester
seijd, wanneer de hulpe van,,
den Mensch mancqueet, als
dan comt de Goddelijcke

101

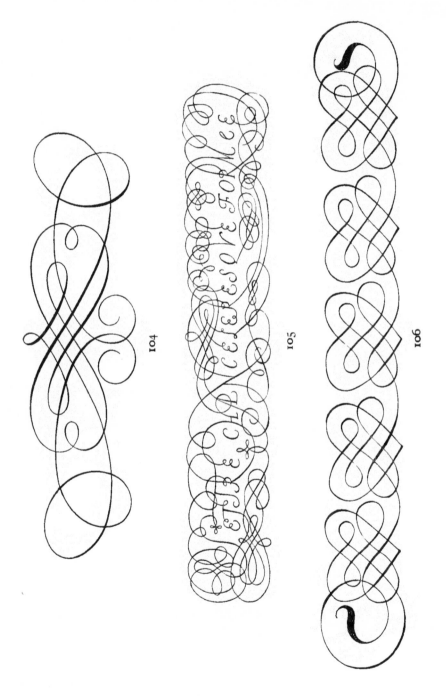

104

105

106

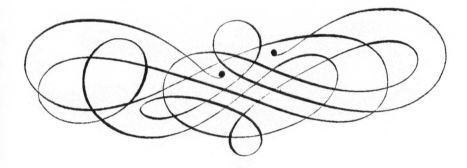

107

108

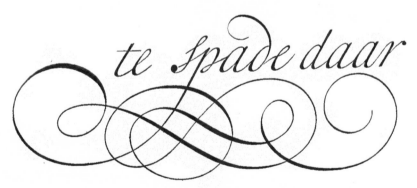

109

A A. a.a.b.b.cc.d.d.e.c.f.g.h.h.i.k.l.m.m.n.n.o.o.o.p.q.r.z.ſ.s.ſſ.ſt.t.tt.u. v. x. y. z ʒʒʒʒʒ

110

111

Richard daniel
1 6 6 3

112

ALPHABETICAL LIST OF AUTHORS

WITH THE NAMES OF THOSE OF THEIR BOOKS WHICH
HAVE BEEN DRAWN UPON FOR ILLUSTRATIONS

ALLAIS DE BEAULIEU, JEAN BAPTISTE.
L'art d'Ecrire ov Le moyen d'exceler en cet Art sans
Maistre.   Paris, 1680.
No. 52.

AMPHIAREO, FRATE VESPASIANO.
Opera di Frate Vespesiano Amphiareo da Ferrara dell'ordine
minore conventvale nella quale si insegna scrivere Varie Sorti di
Lettere, Et Massime Una Lettera Bastarda Da Lui, Novamente,
Con Sua Industria Ritrovata.   Vinegia, 1554.
No. 68.

ANDRADE DE FIGUEIREDO, MANOEL DE.
Nova Escola para aprender A ler, escrever, e contar.   Primeira
Parte.   Lisboa, 1722.
Nos. 64, 86, 87.

AYRES, JOHN.
A Tutor to Penmanship; or, the writing master : a Copy Book
shewing all the Variety of Penmanship and Clerkship as now
practised in England. (2 parts.)   London, 1698.
Nos. 13, 14.

AZNAR DE POLANCO, JUAN CLAUDIO.
Arte Nueva de Escribir por preceptos geometricos, y reglas
mathematicas.   Madrid, 1719.
No. 4.

BAURENFEIND, MICHAEL.
Michael Baurenfeinds   Vollkommene Wieder-Herstellung der
. . . Schreib - Kunst . gezeiget . . . von Christoph Weigel
in Nürnberg.   1716.
No. 85.
P

BEAUCHESNE, J. DE, and BAILDON, JOHN.
A booke containing divers sortes of hands as well the English as
French secretarie with the Italian, Roman, Chancelry and Court
hands. Also the true and iust proportiõ of the capitall Romœ set
forth by J. de Beauchesne P. and M. John Baildon. Imprinted at
London by Thomas Vautroiuillier dwelling in the blackefrieres.

London, 1571.

Nos. 5, 28, 40, 41, 42.

BEAUGRAND, JEAN DE.
Poecilographie Ov diverses escritures propres pour L'Usage
Ordinaire avec une methode fort breve et facile pour les bien
apprendre par Jean de Beaugrand Parisien Secretaire . . . de
la chambre de Roy etc.
Probably published at Paris early in the 17th century.
Nos. 20, 80, 81, 82.

BICKHAM, GEORGE.
The Universal Penman; Or the Art of Writing Made Useful To
the Gentleman and Scholar, as well As the Man of Business . . .
Written With the friendly Assistance of several of the most
Eminent Masters And Engraved by Geo. Bickham. London.

First issued in parts 1733–41, republished 1743.
No. 93.

CASANOVA, JOSEPH DE.
Primera parte del arte de escrivir todas formas de letras por el
Maestro Joseph de Casanova. Madrid, 1650.
Nos. 32, 36.

CHAMBRE, see DE LA CHAMBRE.

CLARK, JOHN.
Writing Improv'd or penmanship made easy, in its useful and
ornamental parts. With various Examples of all the Hands
now Practis'd in Great Britain. Engraved by George Bickham.

London, 1714.
No. 16.

COCKER, EDWARD.
Magnum in Parvo or the Pen's Perfection.
(The copy in the British Museum is dated 1675, but in that
the particular plate illustrated here does not appear.)
No 15.

The Pen's Transcendency: or Fair Writings Store-house Fur-
nished with examples of all the Curious Hands practised in
England and the Nations adjacent.   London, 1660.
No. 96.

CRESCI, GIOVANNI FRANCESCO.
Il perfetto Scrittore Di M. Gio. Francesco Cresci Cittadino
Milanese Doue se veggono i veri Caratteri & le natural forme
di tutte quelle sorti di lettere che à vero scrittor si appartengono.
Con alcun'altre da lui nuouamente ritrouate: Et i modi che
deue tenere il mastro per ben insegnare.   Venetia, 1569.
Nos. 2, 3, 35, 55, 56, 69, 70.

CURIONE, LUDOVICO.
Il Cancelliere di Ludovico Curione ornato di lettere corsiue et
d'altre maniere di caratteri vsati a scriuersi in Italia.   Libro
Quarto.   Roma, 1609.
Nos. 61, 77.

DANIEL, RICHARD.
Daniel's Copy-Book: or A Compendium of the most Usual
Hands of England, Netherlands, France, Spaine, and Italie etc.
                                                London, 1664.

Nos. 50, 90, 91, 92, 112.

DAVIES OF HEREFORD, JOHN.
The Writing Schoolemaster, or the Anatomie of faire writing,
Wherein is exactlie expressed each severall Character. Together
with other Rules and Documents coincident to the Art of Faire
and speedy writing. By John Davies of Hereford. London, 1648.
(There is also a portrait with some title dated 1631.)
No. 62.

DE LA CHAMBRE, JEAN.
Verscheyden geschriften geschreven ende int'Koper gesneden door Jean de la Chambre Liefhebber ende beminder der pennen tot Haarlem. 1638.
Nos. 98, 99.

DESMOULINS, FRANÇOIS.
Le Paranimphe de Lescriture Ronde financière & italienne de nouuelle formes prompte enriches de diuers traictez des inuentions de françois Desmoulins escriuain. Le tout faict & graué par luy mesme. Lyon, 1625.
No. 25.

DIAZ MORANTE, see PALOMARES.

GERY, PETER.
Gerii Viri in Arte Scriptoria quondam celeberrimi opera. Or a copie Book of all the hands now in use Performed according to the naturall Freenes of the Pen by that excellent Mr. of writing Peter Gery. Engraved by Wm. Faithorne. London, 1670.
Nos. 18, 51, 100, 111.

GETHING, RICHARD
Chirographia or A Booke of Copies containing sundrie Examples for such as are desirous to better their hands and attaine to perfection in the Art of commendable Writing, with certaine peeces of Cursorie hands (not heretofore extant) newlie com in vse amongst the gentrie especiallie with secretaries and their Clearks, and are of excellent facilitie and dispatch for any manner of imploiments whatsoever. Composed and published by Richard Gething. 1645.
Nos. 29, 79, 88, 89, 105, 106.

Calligraphotechnia or The Art of faire writing. Sett forth and newly enlarged by Ri: Gethinge Mr: in the said Art dwelling in Fetter-lane, at the hand and Penne, and are to be soulde by George Humble at the white horse in Popes head alley over against the roiall Exchange in London. 1619.
Nos. 95, 107, 108.

HOFMANN, BERTHOLD ULRICH.

Gründliche and leichte Anweissung zur Zierlichen Schreib-Kunst
der lieben Jugend zum besten und auf vielfaltiges Zegehren an
den Tag gegeben von Berthold Ulrich Hofmann Schreib und
Rechenmeister in Nürnberg.   Nürnberg, 1694.
No. 12.

HONDIUS, JODOCUS.

Theatrvm Artis scribendi, Varia Svmmorvm Nostri Seculi,
Artificum exemplaria complectens.   Judoco Hondio celatore.
                                                           1594.
No. 9.

HOUTHUSIUS, JACOBUS.

Exemplaria sive Formulae Scripturae Ornatioris XXXIV. In
quis, praeter diuersa Litterarum genera, varij earumdem ductus
structurae & connexiones.   Antverpia, 1591.
Nos. 8, 19, 43, 44, 45, 58, 110.

LUCAS, FRANCISCO.

Arte de Escrevir de Francisco Lucas Vezino De Sevilla etc.
Dirigada ala S.C.R.M. Del Rey don Phelippe II. Nuestro Señor.
                                                        Madrid, 1577.
Nos. 47, 48.

MATEROT, LUCAS.

Les Oeuvres de Lucas Materot Bovrgvignon François, Citoyen
d'Avignon. Ou lon comprendra facilement la maniere de bien
et proprement escrire toute sorte de lettre Italienne selon l'vsage
de ce siecle.   Avignon, 1608.
Nos. 60, 63, 76.

MORANTE, see PALOMARES.

NEUDOERFFER, JOHANN DER AELTERE.

Anweijsung einer gemeiner hanndschrift. Durch Johann
Neudoerffer, Burger vnd Rechenmeister zu Nurmberg geordnet
und gemacht.   Nürnberg, 1538.
No. 38.

PALATINO, GIOVANNI BATTISTA.

Libro di M. Giovambattista Palatino Cittadino Romano Nelqual s'insegna a Scriuere ogni sorte lettera, Antica et Moderna di qualunque natione con le sue regole et misure et essempi. Et Con vn Breve et Vtil Discorso De Le Cifre: Riueduto nuouamente & corretto dal proprio Autore. Con La Giunta di Qvindici Tavole Bellissime, Romae.   1540.
Nos. 53, 54, 66, 67.

PALOMARES, FRANCISCO XAVIER DE SANTIAGO.

Arte nueva de escribir, inventada por el insigne maestro Pedro Diaz Morante e illustrada con Muestras nuevas, y varios discursos conducentes al verdadero Magisterio de Primas Letras, por D. Francisco Xavier de Santiago Palomares etc.   Madrid, 1776.
Nos. 46, 49, & frontispiece.

PERLINGH, AMBROSIUS.

Exemplaar-Boek Jnhoudende Verscheyde nodige Geschriften . Geschreven en Gesneden, Door Ambrosius Perlingh Schryf-Mr. binnen. . . . Amsterdam.   1679.
Nos. 7, 27, 101, 104, 109.

PERRET, CLEMENT.

Exercitatio Alphabetica nova Et vtilissima Variis Expressa Lingvis et characteribus: Raris ornamentis, vmbris & recessibus picture, Architecturaeque, speciosa, Bruxellae.   1569.
          (Another edition was published by Plantin in 1571.)
Nos. 6, 30, 34, 39, 57.

POLANCO, see AZNAR DE POLANCO.

ROELANDS, DAVID.

t'Magazin Oft'Pac-huys der Loffelycker Penn-const . . . Ghe-practizeert Door David Roelands van Antwerpen, Fransoijschen School-Mr. binnen Vlissinghen.   1616.
Nos. 24, 26, 75, 78, 102.

SCHEURER, GEORG (Publisher, no other name given).

Gründliche Unterricht der edlen Schreib-Kunst in Verlegung Georg Scheurers Kunst-Händlers in Nürnberg.   (No date.)
No. 65.

STOSSEL, JOHANN CHRISTOPH (Publisher, no other name given).

Kunst-richtige so wohl Deutsche als Lateinische Sächsiche Vorschriften bestehend in allerhand Current—Cantzelen—fractur—Verfal-Romanischen Quadrat-Buchstaben und Zugwerk so insgemein in Deutschland in sonderheit aber in oberwehnten Sächsischen Landen am gebrauchlichsten, etc. Franckfurth und Leipzigk bey Johann Christoph Stosseln. 1702.

Nos. 17, 37, 84.

STRICK, MARIA.

Tooneel der loflijcke Schrijfpen Ten dienste van de Constbeminnende Jeucht int licht gebracht Door Maria Strick Fransoysche School-houdende binnen . . . Dolff G'hesneden Door Hans Strick. 1607.

Nos. 22, 23, 59, 73, 74, 94, 97.

VELDE, JAN VAN DEN.

Exemplaer-Boec Jnhoudende alderhande Geschriften zeer bequaem ende dienstelijck voor de Joncheydt onde' allen Liefhebbers der Pennen. Harlem, 1607.

No. 10.

Spieghel Der Schrijfkonste in den welcken ghesien worden veelderhande Gheschriften met hare Fondementen ende onderrichtinghe. Ut ghegeven door Jan van den Velde Fransoysch-School M. binnen Rotterdam. 1605.

Nos. 21, 71, 72, 103.

VESPASIANO, see AMPHIAREO.

VRIES, SYMON DE.

Lust-Hof der Schrijft-Konste. 1619.

No. 11.

WESTON, THOMAS.

Illustrissimo Principi C. Ruperto Comiti Palatino Rheni . . . hoc in Arte Scriptoria Tentamen imperfectum Submisso cultu DDD Tho: Weston. 1681.

No. 83.

WYSS, R.

Libellus valde doctus elegans utilis, multa varia scribendarum litterarum genera complectens. Zürich, 1549.
No. 33.

YCIAR, JUAN DE.

Recopilacion subtilissima: intitvlada Orthographia practica . . Hecho y experimentado por Juã de Yciar Vizcayno, escriptor de libros por la qual se enseña a escrevir perfectamente; ansi por practica como por geometria todas las suertes de letras que mas en España . . . y fuera della se usan . . cortado por J. de Vingles Frances. Caragoça, 1548.
Nos. 1, 31.

A LIST OF Mr. LEWIS F. DAY'S BOOKS
FOR DESIGNERS, Etc.

Alphabets, Old and New. Containing over 200 complete Alphabets, 30 Series of Numerals, and numerous Facsimiles of Ancient Dates. With Modern Examples specially designed by well-known artists. Third Edition, revised and enlarged, with many Illustrations new to this Edition. Crown 8vo, art linen. Price 5s. net.

Lettering in Ornament. An Inquiry into the Decorative Use of Lettering, Past, Present, and Possible. With 200 Illustrations from Photographs and Drawings. Crown 8vo, cloth. Price 5s. net.

Nature and Ornament. Vol. I.—Nature the Raw Material of Design. With 350 Illustrations. Med. 8vo, cloth. Price 5s. net. Vol. II.—Ornament the finished Product of Design. With 600 Illustrations. Med. 8vo, cloth. Price 7s. 6d. net.
These two volumes may be had bound complete in one handsome volume, cloth gilt. Price 12s. 6d. net.

Ornament and its Application. With about 300 full-page and other Illustrations. Large 8vo, cloth gilt. Price 8s. 6d. net.

Pattern Design. With upwards of 300 Illustrations. Large 8vo, cloth gilt. Price 7s. 6d. net.

Windows.—A Book about Stained and Painted Glass. Third Edition, containing 70 full-page Plates and 200 Illustrations in the text. 400 pages. Large 8vo, cloth gilt. Price 21s. net.

Art in Needlework. A Book about Embroidery. Third Edition, revised and enlarged. Containing 81 full-page Plates and 39 Illustrations in the text. Crown 8vo, cloth. Price 5s. net.

Enamelling. With 115 Illustrations. Demy 8vo, cloth gilt. Price 7s. 6d. net.

By Mr. PERCY J. SMITH

Lettering and Writing. A Series of Alphabets and their Decorative Treatment, with Examples and Notes illustrative of Construction, Arrangement, Spacing, and Adaptation of Letters to Materials. Containing 16 Plates in line, printed on stout boards for purposes of Teaching, Study, etc. Large 4to, in case. Price 3s. 6d. net.

Q

A LIST of some REFERENCE BOOKS INDISPENSABLE for DESIGNERS

A Handbook of Ornament. With 3000 Illustrations of the Elements and the Application of Decoration to Objects, systematically arranged according to Subject and Material. By F. S. MEYER, Professor at the School of Applied Art, Karlsruhe. Third English Edition revised by HUGH STANNUS, F.R.I.B.A. Thick demy 8vo, cloth gilt. Price 12s. 6d.

The Styles of Ornament. From Prehistoric Times to the Middle of the XIXth Century. A Series of 3500 Examples. Arranged in Historical Order with Descriptive Text for the use of Architects, Designers, Craftsmen, and Amateurs. By ALEXANDER SPELTZ, Architect. Translated from the Second German Edition. Revised and edited by R. PHENÉ SPIERS, F.S.A., F.R.I.B.A. Containing 650 pages, with 400 full-page Plates. Large 8vo, cloth gilt. Price 15s. net.

A Manual of Historic Ornament. Treating upon the Evolution, Tradition, and Development of Architecture and other Applied Arts prepared for the Use of Students and Craftsmen. By RICHARD GLAZIER, A.R.I.B.A., Headmaster of the Manchester School of Art. Second Edition, revised and enlarged. With 500 Illustrations. Royal 8vo, cloth gilt. Price 6s. net.

The Principles of Design. A Textbook especially designed to meet the requirements of the Board of Education Examination Syllabus on "Principles of Design." By G. WOOLLISCROFT RHEAD, Hon. A.R.C.A. With 16 Photographic Plates, and over 400 other Illustrations, chiefly from line drawings by the Author. Demy 8vo, art linen gilt. Price 6s. net.

An Alphabet of Roman Capitals. Together with Three Sets of Lowercase Letters, selected and enlarged from the finest examples and periods. By G. WOOLISCROFT RHEAD, R.E., Hon. A.R.C.A. Each letter 7 in. square, with descriptive text. In stout wrapper-envelope. Price 2s. 6d. net.

Decorative Plant and Flower Studies. By J. FOORD. Containing 40 Coloured Plates, with a Description and Sketch of each Plant and 450 Studies of Growth and Detail. Imperial 4to, cloth gilt. Price 30s. net.

NOTE.—A Complete List of B. T. Batsford's Publications on Architecture, Decoration, and Furniture, will be sent post free upon application.

B. T. BATSFORD, Publisher, 94 High Holborn, London